Ingredients

Thanks to
Ant Ball, Mike Garry and all the Stars at the Summerhouse
Ian Bobb for cover image and artwork on pages 4, 11, 29
Peter Kalu and all the Commonword Staff
Ric Michael
The infinitie diversity of creativity

The StorM Of The Eye (first rotation)

I am cut from the same cloth you use 2 hide me from your vision
And I'm intent like a starved moth 2 devour the flames of your ignition
I am fed by just one cause and its fulfillment is my nutrition
I am led by just one boss, my god... I call it intuition

I bleed the same red blood so don't pretend like you don't know me
You have spilled the same said blood convinced one day that you could own me
You have pushed me so far down some of my own kind now disown me
But just because you stole my crown that doesn't mean that you've dethroned me

You believe the same damn lies spread by the ones who came b4 you
And though you wear a new disguise still in your eyes I see the core you
So it comes as no surprise when you surprise me with your methods
You claim your jungle is civilized but I see cheaters, snakes and leopards

And though I try not 2 generalize 'cause general eyes see false predictions
Some of you know where justice resides but far 2 few 2 make distinctions
So when you see me roll my eyes don't think they symbolize submission
I've just noticed vultures circling skies feeding off the carcass of tradition

And my first notion is 2 shoot them 'cause they took justice and they raped her
Trace their vines back and uproot them crush the seeds, and kill the propagator
But I'll just clip their wings 'cause I need their eyes 2 see me flourish
Bound by their own historical rings they gorge but still remain malnourished
And I'm not saying that what's happened in the past is not worth knowing
It's just I feel I'm prone 2 trip and fall right on my arse, if I keep looking where I've been
Instead of where I'm going...

1

Angel. (Part 1)

Angel has disowned me,

For I forgot what she had shown me,

So now life has cruelly thrown me

Unto she who inflicts pain.

And still I do feel lonely,

Though the mirrors they do clone me,

Wherever man looks he looks in vain...

The facts of Life

Age & Maturity
don't walk hand in hand.
Wage & Security
seldom meet.
Cage & Authority
both play in a band.
Ignorance & Fear
nod 2 the beat.
Love & Honesty
don't always get along.
The oppressed are far from free
not far from you.
So Justice & Liberation sing the same old song.
A song sung by so many
heard by so few.

The X-Men

We be like those fears that you all have but leave unspoken.
But We be real just like those tears that only cry when hearts are broken.
We be like the sun, we will shine until you see us.
We be wise 2 all those liars who criticise, but wanna be us.
We be like those rules that you dictate b4 you break them.
We be those great ideas that you ignore, then imitate them.
We be like those clues that solve the case that you keep missing.
We be like those tunes you say you hate...but can't stop whistling.
We be like that sex that gives you unrestricted pleasure.
We be the X that marks the spot, that finds the buried treasure.
Yes we be the X-men, but no matter where we try 2 live,
You keep us on the run, just like that man...'The Fugitive'.

But we be like those seeds that grow no matter what the season.
We be real just like those Gods that you all know, but won't believe in.
We burn like those fires that only justice can extinguish.
We come dressed in an attire that only true hearts can distinguish.
We be like that food you swear you hate but never tasted.
We be that phobia that rules your life until you face it.
We be like those visions that you swear are just illusion.
So you keep us in those prisons without walls, that's no solution.
Yes we be the X-men, despised and under-rated.
But after we die the next men will be twice as concentrated.
Yes we be the X-men, should you require further proof...
Look 4 us in the X-files we be out there...like the truth.

On Heat!

I can feel their pressure cooking no!
Simmering my next intention
I can feel all their eyes looking
Even when they're not facing my
direction
I watch letters undress try 2 impress
As they vie 4 my attention
The only way 2 relieve my stress is 2
probe them
With my...lyrical erection
And words that fear my reputation
try their best 2 be discreet
And not 2 tap their shoes
'Cause they know whenever I'm in
lyrical heat
I'm Fucking any word that moves

I hear their breaths inhale as they
stagger
Dizzy with anticipation
I feel reality's wheels derail off
beaten tracks
2 universal destinations

And they recognise a revolution is at
hand when I arise
And become their, exhalation
Then we agree our only limits are the
skies until we reach them
Then move on 2 revelation
But first we exhume the body of
justice and dust off the lies
From the eyes she seldom uses
We're afraid she may be dead until
she smiles and says;
'I have always been alive, just 2 often
buried by mans excuses'

But as we advance and beat off
hypocrites that feed off shit like flies
Wish I were anything but human

'Cause some of those things that they
stand 4 that I despise
I know sometimes...I do them

But Justice trusts that there's more
truth in me than lies And 4 that
reason she allows me 2 lay my head
upon her shoulder as I cry
When my own words try 2 devour
me
But every time justice says jump I
ask high?'
And she says 'Higher than b4'
On a good day I can reach beyond
the sky
But sometimes, I can't even leave
the floor.

TOTEM

five

You
can
not
ever
predict
2
what
extent
it
might
aspire
So
when
curiosity
sparks
a
thought
you'd
best
beware
of
its'
desires
because
within
the
jungle
of
the
mind
sparks
soon
become
forest
fires
!

PeN tip aggression

Should've taught that man a lesson
Should've made him pay the price
Fixed him in-between the jaws of my aggression
And then slowly, squeezed the vice

Should've made that man my subject
Locked him in a cold dark place
And then harassed him like the prime suspect
Of an unsolved murder case

Should've made him an example
Should've made that word his last
Fixed his head upon my mantle
After I'd pulled it through his arse

Could've made that man an ally
Would've made that man a friend
But now his actions ask me shall I...
...Squeeze his neck till his life ends?

Perhaps he's mad with his existence and all the chances that he's missed
If that's the case it's more than his life's worth 2 add me 2 his list

But now he's wound up like a rotary
He'll never know
I could've changed his lifestyle totally
Introduced his mind 2 poetry
Diffused his ticking time bomb... vocally

So now I sit and write in hindsight about what could've been
But isn't
He'll never know how close he came 2 what he could've seen
But didn't

Each time my devils take their aim
I call on angels 2 extinguish
Poisoned arrows doused in flames
That they're just dying 2 relinquish

But instead of pleasing them I take a pen and write a poem
And hope I exorcise the demons that I came so close 2 showing
If he came across these words he'd probably think that I was bluffing
But in face of all his provocation, I command victory when I do nothing

So next time you're faced with choices that entice you 2 abuse them
Remember this;
Your greatest strength is not your words but the patience...2 use them.

One 2 many

Here's 2 those who choose 2 use the pen and not the sword
2 those who only rock the boat 2 throw injustice over board
Here's 2 those who rise above the trials of all oppression
2 those who meet their burdens with a smile and not aggression
But then here's 2 those who choose 2 right the wrongs no one should have 2 see
Let's crush all those who bruise under the light that shines 4 honesty
Here's 2 those who fly in2 the storm 2 seek their destiny
2 those who'd rather die than be enslaved in any territory
Here's 2 those who plan their course through life not me, instead I...
...throw caution 2 the wind and use the force, just like a Jedi
So if the world be like The Empire, then I be like The Rebel Force
And I'll penetrate it's holes so well you'd swear my name was Intercourse
Let's raise a glass and drink 2 those who try 2 make a difference
Then let's kick the arse of those who think 2 threaten our existence
If opportunity smiles let's make a pass and hope that she will kiss us
If the hand of lunacy grabs let's move real fast and pray that he will miss us
Here's 2 those who sacrifice the few 2 save the many
2 those who thought they fought and died 4 me and you, the military
Here's 2 black 'n' white and all those colours in-between
I'm sure that even Martians come in different shades of green
Here's 2 rhyme 'n' reason, without which I wouldn't be here
2 whatever you believe in, 2 whatever makes you see clear
Here's 2 poetry how ever shallow, deep or profound...

...And here's 2 alcohol, the more you drink, the better I sound.

You know Who!

The rules they brought were new 2
our kind
None of our kind knew
That they had plans 2 overrule our
kind
And turn all brown eyes blue
They swore they were the glue 2 man
kind
That nothing else would do
But they be more like common flu 2
mankind
And there's still no cure...aaAACHU!

They deemed themselves the super
mankind
Heroes through and through
Saw us fit 2 shine the shoes of their
kind
But not 2 wear them 2
They labelled us as fools in their
minds
Although it wasn't true
The seeds they planted were so deep
in our minds
That pretty soon, they grew.

So now you think I'm being cruel 2
my kind
When I say nigger 2
But I've just forged a tool out of the
weapon
Made by you
So when you see me acting fool with
my kind
I'm not a threat 2 you
It's when you see me acting cool with
my kind
That you should fear 4 you
But take a closer look and you'll find

Me inside of you
That's why you be the look4 tan kind
When the sun don't shine 2 you.

Now in my search 4 proof
I look 4 clues but I can't see
Tracks that cover up the truth
Always wear bigger shoes than me
Facts discovered are no use
Expose my anger's all they do
Blacks be hangin' from a noose
Or on display like at a zoo

So now I kneel and pray 4 mankind
And hope that it comes true
But I need more than words can say
4 mankind
And more than words can do
Perhaps one day I'll wake
And I'll find everything is new
'Cause I've had all that I can take of
mankind
And all I can take...of you!

Freedom... (take 1)

You said they'd interfere with your plans 4 domination.
These are the words you told me, when I spoke of liberation.

From the cradle 2 the grave
I was 2 be your slave & you my master
Behave or face your rage
I could place no gauge on your disaster
Come 2 you intact
I'd always leave with pieces missing
Be a fool & turn my back
You'd stab me twice & leave me wishing
That we had never met
Or better yet, my life was over
You've fucked with me b4
But that was then, now I'm sober
And now you may not live 2 tell the tale of our relation
The pain & grief you've caused me
Needless 2 say, humiliation
I could kill you now, but then all you've stolen how would I find it
I need you here with me
So when my light shines you'll see, and then be blinded
And so I give this weapon 2 you, though death becomes you I cannot use it
Your fate shall be decided by the gods, I will not choose it
Your future may be my past then you will know my degradation
The NIGGER that once served you.....just rehearsed your termination

Angel. (part 2)

...But still I hold my head up high

And laugh when I wanna cry

Knowing one day I will fly

And meet the man who makes the rain.

For although I still do cheat him

'Tis my destiny to meet him

But if he says that I must leave him

I'll return and start again.

He came from who knows where
made tempers flare with all his teaching.
4 sinners he said prayers
'cause the converted don't need preaching.
He said you'll reap the seeds you sow
though some weeds may grow without you knowing.
It doesn't matter where you're from or where you are
but where you're going.

He never changed his spots he stayed the same just like a leopard.
Though some thought him insane said there be madness in his method.
He had no claim 2 fame except his words made people listen.
Could not care less about your name, your age, your sex or your religion.
This man he points 2 God, says you don't have 2 die 2 see him,
Makes non believers nod, and if I wasn't me, I'd want 2 be him.

It's a quiet day for sinners thought the priest, perhaps the lords work is almost done.
Then, as if it had been there all the time, from the other side, a voice speaks...

...4give me father 4 I have sinned
Just can't seem 2 learn my lesson
Don't even ask how long It's been
Since I had my last confession

If you had seen what I have seen
You'd soon change your profession
If you had been where I have been
You 2 would question heaven

4give me father,
I've committed sins more deadly than the 7
Way beyond the reach of any hymns or psalms
Truth is father, I belong in hell, don't consider me 4 heaven
Because I don't think I'd be met with open arms

So tell me father what the future holds
4 one whose only rule is; no holds barred
Tell me father can you save my soul
Or at least replace this joker 4 an ace card

Quickly father you must intervene
Guide me 2 the light I've seldom seen
Hide me from the night that beckons me
Disguise me from the madness that sections me

4give me father 4 I have sinned
Worse than the horn rimmed creature of bad habit
More often than rabbits produce rabbits
Show me the smallest hand of mischief...and I'll grab it

But I fear now that I've said 2 much
Bless me father with a word...
...Or better yet, a touch
Caress me father...
...With faith enough 2 choke the lies out of the demons you might exorcise

The priest is overwhelmed with sympathetic emotion. Contrary to all rules regarding confession he emerges almost subconsciously from his own box and steps in with the confessor, feeling that in this case, words are not enough. However, whilst he surrounds the confessor with his arms and his compassion, there is more revelation to come...

...Thank you father 4 your warm embrace
But you have failed 2 recognize my face
I am a god just like the one you praise
I 2 have a son who's suffered in many ways

Sent 2 exercise a reign of terror
Make you relish in your ways of error
Accept the blemish that you call existence
...The road 2 my house is paved with no repentance

And though his efforts were unduly spurned
I'm here 2 herald his return
Behold the fuel that makes the fire burn
In the endless duel...
...2 decide which way this world will turn

So hear me father now and recognize
The true god that stands b4 your eyes
B4 long I'll call my son 2 rise
Needless 2 say, don't look up 2 the skies

I have told you father
Things mankind will refuse 2 know
Until you spread the word and tell them so
4 who better than a man of god
2 make all non-believers nod

But alas now father I must go
A dark afterlife requires my glow
But b4 I light my fuse and blow
Remember...
                    ...Better the devil you know

The confessor disappears, leaving the priest alone and dumbfounded, his garments saturated with sweat. He sits now on the other side hoping that the nightmare...was just a dream. He clutches the cross around his neck and whispers; "Forgive me father, 4 I have sinned". A voice from the other side replies; " When was your last confession?"

Hell's Angel

I have seen the Devil
Rumours of his death are over-rated
Beneath the bottom level
His ruthless nature exaggerated.

He holds no bodies captive
No souls are burning 4 redemption
In fact he's quite inactive
Has no disciples, no attention.

See loneliness becomes him, bullies and shoves him in2 submission.
4 him there's no variety, and there is no joy in repetition.

He's been cursed by the wrath of the ruler
Unable 2 feel joy or pain
So by doing the good that makes most men feel proud
He himself has nothing 2 gain.

So here he sits in limbo, suspended
With no means of escape or denial
Cast aside since his natural life ended
Because a miss was as good as a mile.

TOTEM Nine

From
flames
your
love
expose
Every
spitting
spark
is
seething
2
be
fire
Every
pose
you
strike
ignites
circuits
I
rewire
Every
impulse
you
express
sketches
more
pieces
2
admire
Priceless
is
the
masterpiece
framed
by
nothing
but
desire

B4 Love was even Invented

B4 language was ever created
B4 the first word was pronounced
B4 the first pupils dilated
Emotions arrived unannounced

B4 the first spark was ignited
B4 the first ballad was sung
B4 the first cupid was sighted
B4 the first kiss, the first tongue

B4 the first promise was spoken
B4 the first heart skipped a beat
B4 the beast known as lust was
awoken we met
And we danced 2 a different beat

B4 the first ear heard sweet nothings
B4 the first hairs stood on end
B4 the first tears cried
B4 the first tongue-tied
B4 the first poem was penned

B4 Casanova knew passion
B4 the first heartstrings were tugged
B4 sex was even in fashion
B4 the first socket was plugged

We met b4 time was an issue
Perhaps b4 time had intended
B4 mankind even dreamt it
We'd signed, sealed and sent it...

B4 the first rose was delivered
B4 the first eyes ever met
B4 the first inner thighs quivered
B4 dry virgin lands, were made wet

B4 the first candlelit dinner
B4 the first vows were exchanged
B4 the first sin had a sinner
B4 the first life had an age...

...B4 the first knee ever bended
B4 the moon gave the sea it's first
wave
B4 the first sunrise ascended
B4 the first death had a grave

We met b4 time was an issue
Perhaps b4 time had intended
B4 mankind even dreamt it
We'd signed, sealed and sent it...

...B4 love was even invented.

Superman

Come fly with me my dear & leave your past behind you.
You'll be safe my dear within these arms of steel.
No-one understands my dear like you do
just how much this man of steel can feel.

It's been so long my dear since I have known tranquillity.
These super ears my dear they hear nothing but screams.
These super eyes my dear they've seen things you don't wanna see.
This open mind has left a trail of open dreams.

For so long my dear to them I've been a saviour.
But oh how wrong they'd be if they could read my mind.
Obligation overshadowed true behaviour.
Come fly with me my dear let's leave this human-kind.

New kid's On the Block!

When Cupid draws his bow, wise men lie low
They've learned their lesson
The star-gazed new kid steals the show he thinks he knows
But he's just guessing.

When Cupid takes his aim wise men refrain from their advances
Curiosity knows no shame the new kid stays, and takes his chances.

When Cupids' arrow flies it cuts through skies of stormy weather
The new kid's not surprised 'cause in her eyes he sees, forever.

When Cupid takes the reins wild hearts are tamed, and then relinquished
Cupid lights a flame the hardest rain could not...extinguish.

Non-believers set the pace Cupid gives chase, and always catches
When Cupids' lighter's out of fuel it's cool, he also carries matches.

When Cupid rings his bell fighters do well, if they've had training
New kids kiss and tell spill all the words they should be..saving.

When Cupid casts his spell you might as well rename him Merlin
'Cause loves cauldron burns like hell when Cupid throws a boy and girl in.

But the new kid's doing well you just can't tell with these beginners
True love it has a way of making good men out of sinners.
Infatuation has a way of making losers think they're winners
But true love never goes off the boil instead it always..simmers.

Master of disguise, one size fits all, always in fashion
Known 2 specialise in fighting lies and crimes of passion

So when Cupid's on the case he leaves no space 4 speculation
Cuts right 2 the chase exposes truth or fabrication.

So b4 you bring your case 2 trial be sure you know what truth is
Because a miss is as good as a mile if love betrays the new kid.

The Frog Prince

A fate that's worse than death I have endured
But now I must reveal I loved my life b4
So now release me from this spell inflict, the cure
So that I might be the frog I was once more
I fail 2 see how you could not resist me
Frankly I fail 2 see how you could think me princely
I was a handsome frog until you kissed me
And then around your selfish love you tried 2 twist me
It's true that all that glistens isn't gold now
But sometimes it doesn't even want 2 be
And if you'd listened very closely you'd have known now
'Cause you'd have heard me scream 'Oh please God no not me.'
So though you've changed me and now dress me like a civilian
These clothes on my true guise I would look silly in
See the truth is dear I'm really an amphibian
You must have chose the one frog in a million.

Blade Men

Wouldn't call us weak men, we just never swam against the tide
The type of men women might seek after a stormy relationship ride
Wouldn't call us meek men we just fell b4 our pride
More afraid 2 unleash the wrath of our own demons caged inside
Never saw us as the right men they just saw an easy ride
They were wolves and we were sheep men they'd say 'jump' we'd ask 'how high?
Walk all over wipe your feet men, background beat men on the side
That's what they saw when they saw these men but these men they saw their brides.

Could never call us stage men all our best lines went unheard
We were more like poetry on the page men so you could never comprehend our words
Wouldn't call us slave men we just did as we were told
Bust your arse 4 minimum wage men never cast in starring roles
Wouldn't call us insecure men just unsure men but never faking
Held open doors but we weren't doormen we were your men 4 the making

Wouldn't call us full fledged rage men, can't be phased men's more defining
But when demons unlock cages with their own keys, they're past confining
And if you trample inconsiderately through the mindfield of devotion
Eventually, inevitably, you'll trip the live wire...the explosion

Now we be can't take no more when pushed 2 far men...we push back
From peaceful life 2 war men, ripe 2 raw men, fade 2 black...

Still...wouldn't call us 12 bore gauge men, we could never be so loud
We be more like small sharp discreet...blade men, hardly noticed in a crowd
And those be the weapons that we chose when 2 strangers schemed the perfect crime
2 relieve each other of our burdens, I'd kill his wife...he'd kill mine...

Snake

Compare me not 2 a bird 4 I cannot fly and I cannot sing.

Compare me not 2 an angel, 4 every day I am guilty of sin.

Compare me not 2 a flower 4 I do not smile with the rising sun.

Compare me not 2 a clown, 4 I am not notorious 4 having fun.

Compare me not 2 a criminal, not a murderer or a thief although,

The wealthiest of the wealthy would find my riches beyond belief.

Compare me instead 2 a creature, so often misunderstood.

Just because I'm ugly does not mean that I'm not good.

Just because I crawl along the ground don't mean 2 say,

That misfortune falls upon whomever dares 2 come my way.

But if you should come 2 me and leave with nothing but hurt and shame.

Then just as I have brought you sorrow, only I can ease your pain.

The Mocking Bird

His name and fame preceded him
Way b4 his first arrival
His skills by far exceeded
All his piers and all his rivals

Once this was a chore 4 him
Necessary 4 survival
But now the thrill was in the chase
4 him
The catch, no longer vital

It's been that way 4 years
No fear of consequences after
So when challenged he'd cry tears
Distilled through mocking, heartless
laughter

Ended potential predator careers
B4 they even had a chance
4 his chosen prey, certain death
Disguised by beautiful advances

So now we catch him on his,
'retirement' day
Embellishing stories of his...*romances*;

"Yes folks it's always been this way
Survival of the fittest
The early bird that chooses 2 seize
the day
Catches the worms that grow the
biggest"

Yeah the bird that always got the
worm
Was braggin' 'bout his conquests
"You youngsters got a lot 2 learn
B4 you get the medals on my chest"

Now one bird was known as
'Bookworm'
'Cause all he ever did was read
About great birds that came b4 him
And how they satisfied their...greed

And when the bird that always got the
 worm
Came 2 the end of his recital
'Bookworm' raised one wing above his
head and said
"Excuse me sir but I've just read
Most worms are suicidal"!

The Twelfth Messenger (act one)

Our opening scene finds the king reclining in his throne, talking to himself, recognising the error of his ways and seeking to make amends. A menacing shadow of a large henchman stands to his right.

A better man than this I was 4 sure
Until I was overcome by thoughts, impure
If I could have one wish I'd beg a cure
Although I feel I'd need not one but 3 or 4
Now I've learned my lessons well
Stories 2 tell yes I have plenty
Sold my soul 2 hell because the needs of the one
Outweighed the needs of the many.
Placed myself b4 her, swore I adored her
I was lying
Now I'd lay my life b4 her, do anything for her, pledge love
undying.
The storm b4 the calm that's all it was but now it's over
Eccentric wit and charm that never worked when I was sober
I have but one request dare I be blessed with her 4giveness....

He is interrupted nearing the end of his..realisation, by his henchman who bellows;

"SIRE, THE TWELFTH MESSENGER APPROACHES".

The king replies;
"You know what 2 do"

Messenger makes his way towards stage, greeted by an intense silence. The kings' executioner prepares his weapon as the king locks eyes with the messenger.
Could there be a glimmer of hope in his eyes?
The king interjects as his henchman is about to slit the messenger's throat;

"WAIT, don't kill this messenger perhaps he brings good news
could be the driver of the passenger that might relieve my blues
Like 'Macgyver'* he's the one that could rewire or defuse
the affections 4 my true love that might serve 2 change her views

*Late 80's US series

25

Wait, don't kill this messenger he brings with him an aura
I feel this time might be the last time that I have 2 grovel 4 her
If persistence were a crime I'd be in jail doing time 4 her
She's the reason the sun shines and I've been obsessed since I first saw her.
So come forth young messenger, hand over the note
and pray the kiss she blows this time will be enough 2 float my boat....."

The trembling figure advances and tentatively outstretches his arm...
The king snatches and unwraps the note.
He does not avert his eyes from the messenger until he begins to read...
(voice of his true love is heard).

My dearest Fidel,

4 each other we were meant 2 be
that was my intuition
Not just a lover but a friend 2 me
a perfect composition
In a world cursed with monotony
a match made in distinction
Yes once we shared a chemistry
In that there is no fiction.

Fidel casts a favourable glimpse at the messenger, then reads on...

Now I fear there is no remedy that eases this affliction
All the words you ever said 2 me are lost in contradiction
Eleven messengers you've sent 2 me
Eleven times I've wrote this
Still you send a twelfth 2 me
I hope this time you'll notice.

I would say this face-2-face 2 you
But my body would betray me
All my morals fall from grace 2 you
All my No's turn into Maybes

Though in my heart there is a place 4 you
In my book, more than one chapter
The thrill is in the chase 4 you
No interest after capture
Hope this messenger makes haste 2 thee
Before you send another
We can be friends at best platonically
But we will not again be lovers...

**Again there is an intense silence, much more impending than the last.
The kings disappointment is apparent, his anger, immense.
After messenger number 8 had again brought a similar response, the
king had dispensed with reading the replies brought to him by 9, 10 and
11, he had simply had his henchman murder them, pre-empting their
bad tidings. Now he had allowed the 12th messenger to fool him with a
positive gaze therefore prolonging his life and wasting the kings efforts.
Question- what does a king do, when killing the messenger doesn't
seem enough?
Silence, as the king, seething, gathers himself just long enough to expel
the following words;**

Wait, there must be a mistake
These words cannot be meant 4 me
This note must be a fake
Because her logic makes no sense 2 me
2 late 2 use the brakes
Now I've been driven through insanity WAIT...

Don't just kill the messenger...
...Kill his whole damn fuc#ing family.

**King dismisses messenger to his doom, he pleads for his loved ones to
be spared.
The king snatches a sheet of clean paper, laughs insanely and starts
to write...**

The end?

The Body Snatchers

They are in disguise
When all the while you thought you knew them
They appear in human guise
But if you look real close, you can see right through them
They penetrate your mind
That's how they know so much about you
There they mature like vintage wine
Fermenting negatives 2 doubt you
It's always a surprise
And it always hurts when they betray you.
Their true colours are inside
And only show when they've enslaved you.

But now I'm almost one of them and It's so damn hard 2 fight this.
Almost one of them, so I just have time 2 write this;

2 whom it may concern
If you should ever find this notice
From these words I hope you'll learn
I was like you before I wrote this

Don't look 2 the skies
'Cause they won't come from up above you,
But you will know when they arrive
Because they always say...

...I LOVE YOU

Enemy Within

Enemy is here,

I feel his presence, I smell his odour.

My only friend is fear,

Death may be near 4 this young soldier.

I have both eyes 2 see him,

Though I feel I need not use them.

4 2 defeat him I must be him

All his choices, I must choose them.

The darkness amplifies the raging blood that flows within me.

The time is now or never, hesitation will surely kill me.

Morning Dues (911)

We ruin our own lives through our
own lack of intervention
Twist all our own knives right through
the back of best intentions
Tighten the jaws 2 our worst vices till
they leave damaging impressions
Sharpen the claws that scratch our
backs till they open wounds that crave
infection

We look 4 tears in eyes of laughter
Indulge in fears that we expose
Destroy the things we cannot master
Never search 4 the friend within
our foes

We cherish things that have no
meaning
Embellish gods with our own rules
Choose infertile ground 2 breed our
young
Then blame their outcome on our
schools

It seems we hear but never listen
Tap our feet 2 the wrong rhythm
Practice religion and blasphemy with
hypocritical precision
And because we found them guilty,
criminals languish in our prisons
Although we may not share their
methods, they're still human...
so we all share their convictions

But despite all of natures' warnings,
we refuse 2 take her remedies
And believe we know what's best
when we've been blind 4 fucking
centuries

But by the time we realise that we've
been fighting the wrong enemies
We'll effect our own demise and eat
the dirt in our own cemeteries.

I've ruined my own life through my
own lack of intervention
Twisted my own knife right through
the back of best intentions
Tightened the jaws 2 my worst vices
till they left damaging impressions
Sharpened the claws that scratched
my back till they opened wounds that
craved infection

But now I'm left in this inferno 2
contemplate my next direction
Be cremated alive or head 4 the
window 4 a crash course flying lesson
And when the news reports of the
pain and grief that terrorists inflicted
They'll say innocent people died here,
 but I don't think they ever existed
So as a crumbling concrete curtain
crashes down and crushes countless
sorry lives
I take my final bow
And put away the mobile phone
'Fuck it!'
'ts between me and my maker now

Eyes wide shut

I never saw it coming
Though I always knew that it was there
But like the sound of distant drumming
It could have been coming from anywhere
It's not that I was running, or afraid 2 meet it's stare it's just...
It took me by surprise, and I didn't think that it would dare

But don't cry 4 me, it was time 4 me, despite what the doctors said
Although my eyes are open wide...

I'm dead.

The Pieces In-between

The knowledge between the question and the answer
The rhythm between the music and the dancer
The distance between 2 fighters b4 they close it
The thought the writer conjured but never wrote it

The eye contact between the sniper and his target
The common ground between the fiction and the fact
The sound b4 the stock exchange opens the market
The clarity b4 addiction takes you back

The moment just b4 2 lovers say those 3 words
The spaces in-between performance and applause
When the cup that I thought was half empty still quenches my thirst
The knowing smiles on faces I thought my words had lost

The lessons I learn between instinct and instruction
The path between the professional and the beginner
The virgins' final stop b4 corruption
The road between the good man and the sinner

When I accept that the shoe fits, then wear it proudly
When I'm as graceful in my rise and in my fall
The deadly sin that searched but never found me
The deadly sin that rose each time I *chose* 2 call

The gaps that fill the spaces between emotions
The wake that frees the reality of the dream
The magic that still works *without* the potion
The peace is in the pieces in-between.

TOTEM eight

Outside
prisons
of
the
mind
that's
where
you'll
find
them
running
riot
Unquestioned
answers
taunting
making
inquisition
their
only
diet
Unraveling
binds
that
tie
bending
bars
releasing
'convicts'
shhh
Listen
hear
them
cry
*'No
Creation
Without
Conflict'*

Party in the Penthouse Suite (No invitation required)

Troubles they get lonely, so they come 2gether.
Good times are content so they come alone.
Addiction brings whoever gives him momentary pleasure.
Intention leaves his best laid plans at home.

Sincerity brings the host his favourite beverage.
Fidelity drinks a toast 2 loyalty.
Integrity's still intact and seems 2 never age.
Ego struts around like royalty.

Eagerness comes 2 early and has 2 wait awhile.
Indecision comes, then leaves and then returns.
Religion tries 2 mingle then meets Temptation and Denial
And has since 4gotten everything he'd learned.

Insecurity shows up late, heads straight 4 the bathroom.
Didn't really anticipate so many guests.
Anticipation's overdressed soon re-dressed by Reality.
And Vanity well she just can't be impressed.

Profanity's being rude can't help the way he's speaking.
But Lust is always there 2 lend an ear.

Insanity's in the nude, that's how she came in, streaking.
Even Awareness can't control when she appears.

Devotion comes and overstays her welcome.
Till Promiscuity comes and grabs her by the waist.
Greed has brought some weed and tries 2 sell some.
Or maybe Need is what necessitates his ways.

Emotions they run wild up in the penthouse suite.
Where life's no masquerade or fancy dress.
Where Indulgence is most welcome and most indiscreet
And where notions in disguise are soon undressed.

Armies of conscience (Part 1)

Tried their clothes on once or 2wice b4 but never really thought they suited me
Encountered foes not unlike these b4 so this war was nothing new 2 me

This time the general wore a smile as if he had a brand new strategy
Like I wouldn't recognise his style from the last time he tried recruiting me

I must admit it's been a while since his foot soldiers last caught up with me
His last words, always the same; 'You can run, but you can't hide from me'

And so they find me in the places that I visit oh so frequently
And catch me playing aces when opponents are just not worthy
They watch me running races led and driven by futility
Then they remind me there's no future in the faces of hypocrisy

But they know that I'm not new 2 this so they offer me no sympathy
They simmer like the catalyst that's poised 2 change my chemistry
Glimmer like the sparks that light the tunnels of insanity
Shimmer like the armour worn, by the soldiers of integrity.

In-'ected'. (About the author)

Bless-ed are those who believe me.
Curs-ed are those who do not.
Tested are those who refuse 2 believe that this life,
Is not all they've got.
Rejected are those who deceive me.
Retested are those who repent.
Respected are those who chose not 2 believe what I said,
But knew what I meant.
Detested are those who enslaved me.
Infected are those who agree.
Disconnected are those who impose on my nature
And question my right 2 be me.
Inspected are those who befriend me.
Selected are those who are true.
Detected are those dressed in clothes 2 disguise their dishonesty
And try 2 get through.
Resurrected are the foes who proved worthy.
4 what good is this life without trial
But never-ending be the power that serves me.
So in the face of my enemy, I smile.

The StorM Of The Eye (final rotation)

...I breath life 2 words on page that keep you engaged through all conditions
Release reality from a cage forged by love, rage and religion
Violate you sexually with a tool sharpened by your lust and indecision
Penetrate you mentally at the school where the only rule is; shut up and listen
If you've not heard this b4 well now you know what you've been missing
Prostituting words on page like whores who fu#k but don't do kissing
Words be powerful like Samson or downright cunning like Delilah
Could take you centuries 2 fathom or just a moment 2 decipher
Similes and metaphors fight 4 the cause or cause the fighting
Holding keys that open doors or open wounds when I be writing
Crossing I's and dotting T's just 2 make shit more exciting
Sailing verbal seas with ease through all degrees no compromising
And you thought you'd paid your fees 2 hear me poetry recite
When in fact it seems you've paid 2 watch a madman's fuse ignite
And when it blows who knows perhaps we'll take our rightful place again
Because the paths that you choose 4 us always lead 2 a dead end
But we keep appearing like the chorus of a song that has no end
Until you realise the foe that you fear the most is your only friend
So you can choose your path, you can choose your sins and which god sees them
But when you choose your path be prepared 2 face the wrath of your own demons
'Cause whatever happens next whether in this text or not was meant 2 be
'Cause only half the path is chosen, the other half is destiny
And you thought you'd paid your fees 2 hear me poetry recite
When in fact it seems you've paid 2 watch a madman's fuse ignite
And when it blows who knows perhaps we'll take our rightful place again
Just like it was at the beginning...so it shall be at the end.

Sixth Sense

See me now through eyes you've never used b4 then never doubt or ask me how just know there's always something more than meets the I am not the man you came here 4 and I will never be not even 4 a second If your bottles wash upon my shore don't be sure you'll get the answers that you beckoned **Feel** me now with hands that never touched the core or brushed the surface whilst you drown under the pressure of your piers b4 you let the individual surface **Hear** me now with ears that always heard the truth but never listened Feel the uncompromising heat radiate from stars after their light has been imprisoned The same heat will melt the bars ignite the lies that still reside in you then the same light that lit your way will become the same light that will be blinding you But **smell** me now through noses blown and recognise my true aroma **Touch** my brow then **taste** the sweat from carrying your chips upon my shoulders Then know you aint seen nothing yet cos chips can't help but become boulders don't think you've extinguished all your debt because smoke still rises...fires still smoulder.